BROADWAY SONGS FOR TWO

Arrangements by Peter Deneff

ISBN 978-1-5400-1283-8

HAL•LEONARD®

7777 W. BLUEMOUND RD. P.O. BOX 13819 MILWAUKEE, WI 53213

Visit Hal Leonard Online at
www.halleonard.com

CONTENTS

ANY DREAM WILL DO

from JOSEPH AND THE AMAZING TECHNICOLOR® DREAMCOAT

FLUTES

Music by ANDREW LLOYD WEBBER
Lyrics by TIM RICE

BRING HIM HOME
from LES MISÉRABLES

FLUTES

Music by CLAUDE-MICHEL SCHÖNBERG
Lyrics by HERBERT KRETZMER
and ALAIN BOUBLIL

CABARET

from the Musical CABARET

FLUTES

Words by FRED EBB
Music by JOHN KANDER

EDELWEISS
from THE SOUND OF MUSIC

FLUTES

Lyrics by OSCAR HAMMERSTEIN II
Music by RICHARD RODGERS

FOR FOREVER

from DEAR EVAN HANSEN

FLUTES

Music and Lyrics by BENJ PASEK
and JUSTIN PAUL

HELLO, DOLLY!

from HELLO, DOLLY!

FLUTES

Music and Lyric by
JERRY HERMAN

15

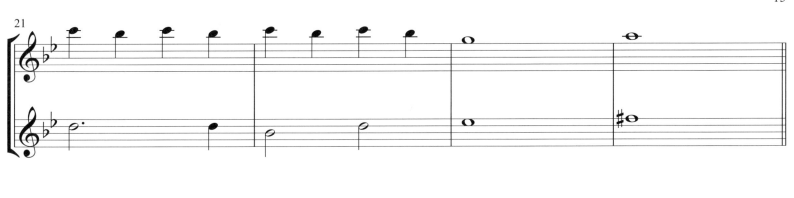

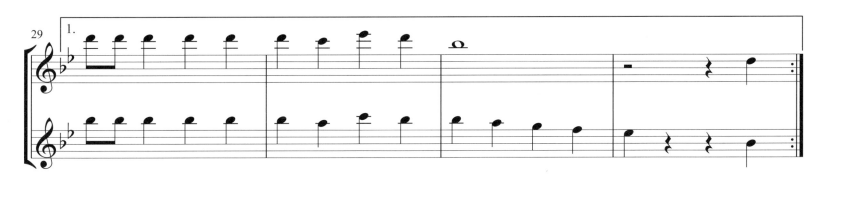

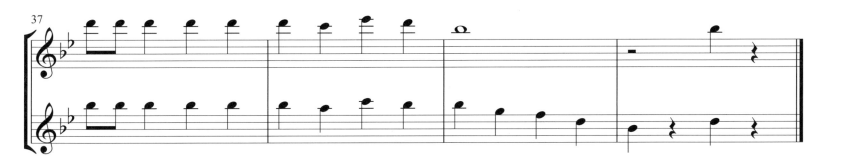

I BELIEVE

from the Broadway Musical THE BOOK OF MORMON

FLUTES

Words and Music by TREY PARKER,
ROBERT LOPEZ and MATT STONE

I WHISTLE A HAPPY TUNE

from THE KING AND I

FLUTES

Lyrics by OSCAR HAMMERSTEIN II
Music by RICHARD RODGERS

IF I WERE A BELL

from GUYS AND DOLLS

FLUTES

By FRANK LOESSER

THE IMPOSSIBLE DREAM
(The Quest)
from MAN OF LA MANCHA

FLUTES

Lyric by JOE DARION
Music by MITCH LEIGH

MAMMA MIA
from MAMMA MIA!

FLUTES

Words and Music by BENNY ANDERSSON,
BJÖRN ULVAEUS and STIG ANDERSON

MEMORY

from CATS

FLUTES

Music by ANDREW LLOYD WEBBER
Text by TREVOR NUNN after T.S. ELIOT

Slowly, with feeling

MY FAVORITE THINGS

from THE SOUND OF MUSIC

FLUTES

Lyrics by OSCAR HAMMERSTEIN II
Music by RICHARD RODGERS

ONE

from A CHORUS LINE

FLUTES

Music by MARVIN HAMLISCH
Lyric by EDWARD KLEBAN

POPULAR

from the Broadway Musical WICKED

FLUTES

Music and Lyrics by
STEPHEN SCHWARTZ

SEASONS OF LOVE
from RENT

FLUTES

Words and Music by
JONATHAN LARSON

Moderately

SEVENTY SIX TROMBONES

from Meredith Willson's THE MUSIC MAN

FLUTES

By MEREDITH WILLSON

SUMMERTIME

from PORGY AND BESS®

FLUTES

Music and Lyrics by GEORGE GERSHWIN,
DuBOSE and DOROTHY HEYWARD
and IRA GERSHWIN

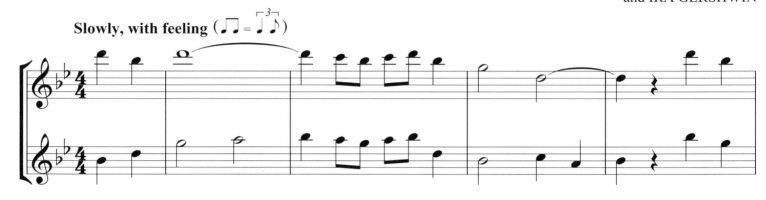

SUNRISE, SUNSET
from the Musical FIDDLER ON THE ROOF

FLUTES

Words by SHELDON HARNICK
Music by JERRY BOCK

TOMORROW
from the Musical Production ANNIE

FLUTES

Lyric by MARTIN CHARNIN
Music by CHARLES STROUSE

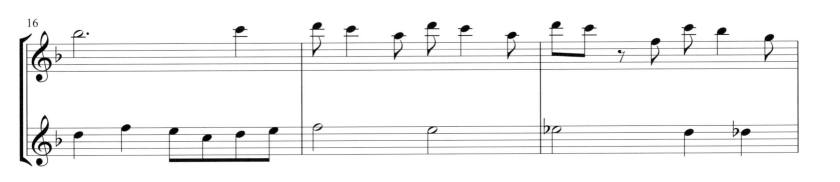

WHERE IS LOVE?

from the Broadway Musical OLIVER!

FLUTES

Words and Music by
LIONEL BART

YOU'VE GOT A FRIEND

featured in BEAUTIFUL: THE CAROLE KING MUSICAL

FLUTES

Words and Music by
CAROLE KING

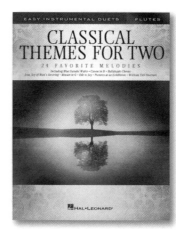